WHITSTABLE NATIVES

The story of the Whitstable oyster

Written by Michael Cable

Photographed by Brian Aris

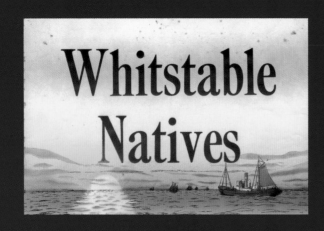

'The poor Britons, there is some good in them after all. They produce an oyster!'

Roman historian Sallust (50 BC)

Whitstable's Native charm 2000 years of history

Whitstable has many claims to fame, some of them quite unexpected. The seascape artist Turner was drawn there by the spectacular sunsets. George Stephenson built the railway from Whitstable to Canterbury that provided the world's first ever regular passenger service when it opened in 1830. And it was a Whitstable man who invented the deep-sea diving suit, testing out his prototype in the bay. But long before all that, of course, it was the oyster – with a little bit of help from Julius Caesar – that first put this short stretch of the Kent coastline firmly on the world map.

Shortly after Caesar's conquest of Britain in 55 BC, the Roman historian Sallust grudgingly conceded: "The poor Britons, there is some good in them after all. They produce an oyster!"

Two thousand years later, Whitstable is still successfully managing to exploit the happy coincidences of geology that created an environment in a few square miles of its shallow inshore waters in which the Native oyster – Ostrea edulis, to give it its correct Latin name – thrives. It also provides the distinctive flavour and texture of the Native that are as familiar to the expert palate as a vintage Puligny

The Whitstable oyster fleet in full sail. Although the Native oyster is making a comeback, there are only four traditional smacks still on the water

Montrachet or Petrus would be to a connoisseur of fine wines.

Although celebrated in art and literature by everyone from Chaucer to Byron, from Dickens to Hemingway and from Manet to Braque, the oyster remains something of an acquired taste. King James I voiced a thought that has probably occurred to most of us at one time or another with his reported observation that: "He was a very valiant man who first adventured on eating oysters."

Whoever it was who first risked slicing his fingers open in an effort to prise apart the razor-sharp shell, and who then dared to swallow the contents, he must have been a very distant ancestor. Archaeological evidence suggests that primitive hunter-gatherers were already enjoying smoked oysters at least 8,000 years ago.

But it was the Romans who first elevated the humble mollusc to the status of a gourmet delight. It appears that no feast or orgy was complete without a plentiful supply of what was even then regarded as a delicacy, with interesting aphrodisiac qualities. Notorious as one of history's greatest gluttons, the Emperor Vitellius was said to have been in the habit of slurping his way through as many as a thousand at a single sitting.

To cater for this sort of demand, a shrewdly entrepreneurial individual named Sergius Orata, credited by Pliny with the invention of the hot shower, also created the world's first artificial oyster beds in the Lucrine Lake, near modern Naples, as early as 95 BC.

However, the more discerning gourmets of the day soon identified the plump, firm-fleshed, nutty-flavoured variety from the Kentish flats as being among the best to be found anywhere in the Empire – one small consolation, perhaps, for what one can imagine might well have been a rather unpopular posting to chilly Britannica.

Gnaeus Julius Agricola grew to like the local Native oysters so much during his seven year stint as Governor between 78 – 85 AD that he arranged to have regular supplies exported back to his friends in Rome.

Slaves were sent out to collect what were then known as 'Rutupians' from natural beds in the vicinity of Reculver, just along the coast from Whitstable and these were shipped back to Rome

from the port of Richborough, packed in sacks of snow to keep them fresh.

Quantities of distinctive English shells recovered by archaeologists from Roman ruins – some of which were even found to include special refrigeration chambers built into cave-like cellars – attest to a well-organised and flourishing trade.

With the end of the Roman occupation and the onset of the Dark Ages, the fashion for oysters in Anglo-Saxon Britain vanished along with mosaic flooring, central heating, flush toilets and all the other sophistications of villa life. We hear very little about oysters from then until the end of the 15th century, by which time the beds at Whitstable were already being farmed on an organised basis.

This becomes clear from a detailed adjudication of the Privy Council which, in 1490, was brought in to settle a boundary dispute between the Lordships of Whitstable and Milton over "ye dredging of Oysters", an early indication of the sort of turf wars that were still causing problems as recently as 1998. At the same time, the Council laid down rules for the protection of the beds, stipulating, among other things, that young brood should be returned there to mature, and also setting a closed season lasting from May 1st to August 1st.

The Whitstable Oyster Fishery Company is still farming those beds to this day, directly supplying its own three restaurants with what are claimed to be the only true Royal Whitstable Native oysters. One of the oldest public companies still in existence in this country, it can trace its origins back to "time immemorial", a phrase that regularly crops up in archive material relating to the ancient rights of the medieval Company of Free Fishers and Dredgers of Whitstable.

This was a forerunner of the great trade and craft guilds, a 'fraternity' or 'corporation' in which the fishermen banded together to form a body through which apprentices were admitted and every aspect of the local oyster dredging industry could be regulated and controlled. It was from this that the modern Whitstable Oyster Fishery Company gradually evolved.

'a great fisher towne...
ther about they dragg
for oysters'

WHITSTABLE OYSTER FISHERY COMPANY.

OFFICES AND STORE

WHITSTABLE OYSTER FISHERY COMPANY.

INTERIOR OF STORE

By the middle of the 16th century, the Kent historian Leland was describing Whitstable as "a great fisher towne of one paroche", adding: "Ther about they dragg for oysters". Meanwhile, demand was once again growing in all the right places.

In April 1589, Sir Francis Walsingham, Queen Elizabeth I's trusted minister and spymaster, on learning that the Queen would be descending on him at his home at Barnelmes, Essex, for a few days during the course of a Royal Progress around the country, wrote to the bailiffs at Colchester, where the oyster beds rivalled those of Whitstable. His urgent request was for some of their fine oysters "for my better provision to enterteyne Her Majestie".

Further evidence of the growing popularity of oysters at this time can be deduced from the frequent references to them by Shakespeare – in King Lear, Anthony and Cleopatra, Richard II, Much Ado About Nothing, The Taming of the Shrew and in Act II Scene II of The Merry Wives of Windsor, where Pistol, in conversation with Falstaff, coins the phrase "the world's mine oyster".

The oyster fishery in Whitstable grew steadily throughout the 17th and 18th centuries until, by 1790, a fleet of around 70 smacks was operating out in the bay. The oyster grounds at this time were still owned by the Lord of the Manor, Viscount Lord Bolingbroke, but he was forced to sell them to a local landowner in order to pay off debts and a couple of years later they were acquired by the Company of Free Fishers and Dredgers.

The Company was duly incorporated by Act of Parliament in 1793, a key development commemorated on the plaque that adorns one end of the old Royal Native Oyster Stores building at the Horsebridge, which now houses the Whitstable Oyster Fishery Company's celebrated fish restaurant.

During the next 100 years, the Company grew steadily, reaching a peak between 1850 and 1865. By then, around 300 dredgermen were working more than 100 smacks, and sending as many as 80 million oysters to Billingsgate a year, earning the Company an annual income of around £90,000. The dredgermen themselves earned up to £5 a week each, very good money indeed in those days.

Built by the
Whitstable Fishing
Company at its yard
on Island Wall in
1890, the yawl
Favourite was sold to
the Whitstable Oyster
Fishery Company in
1918. She was still
working up until
1944, when she was
machine- gunned by
a German aircraft as
she rode at her
moorings. In 1977,
the Favourite Trust
was formed to
restore and preserve
her and she is now
on display just along
the beach from the
Royal Native Oyster
Stores

No surprise, then, that at the Duke of Cumberland, where the dredgermen would regularly assemble in an upstairs room for meetings at which the proceeds from Billingsgate would be shared out, the sounds of "joyous" singing often went on "up to a late hour of the night".

With the neighbouring Seasalter & Ham and Faversham companies and their rivals on the Essex coast operating at the same sort of level, it becomes easier to understand how it was that cheap, abundant oysters became the fast-food fad of the 19th century, on sale for just a few pence per dozen.

In The Pickwick Papers, Charles Dickens conjures up the image of oyster stalls, like modern hot-dog stands, on every street corner in London's East End. He has Sam Weller telling Mr Pickwick: "It's a wery remarkable circumstance, sir, that poverty and oysters always seem to go together." He goes on to add: "Look here, sir; here's an oyster stall to every half-dozen houses. The streets lined vith 'em. Blessed if I don't think that ven a man's wery poor, he rushes out of his lodgings and eats oysters in reg'lar desperation."

As the mid-century boom years continued, Whitstable itself expanded rapidly. In 1859, an article in the magazine All The Year Round, edited at that time by Charles Dickens, described the line of "squat wooden houses, made soot-black with pitch... dwarfed huts on this stony beach" in which most of the dredgermen lived. But by 1870 the population was growing fast and terraces of new brick houses were springing up around the harbour that had been built in 1832, two years after the railway was opened, largely to facilitate the import of coals from Newcastle.

Meanwhile, in 1856, one Richard 'Leggy' Wheeler, skipper of a smack called Bubbles, had opened Wheelers Oyster Bar in the town. This was later taken over by a Mr and Mrs Walsh, who decided to keep the name Wheelers and whose son, Bernard, born in one of the upstairs rooms, went on in 1929 to open a London branch in Old Compton Street.

Today, nearly 150 years after it first opened, the Whitstable restaurant is still there in its original High Street premises. It has

been run for many years now by Delia Fitt, a native of the town herself and a shareholder in the Whitstable Oyster Fishery Company, who says she has been opening oysters since she was 10 years old.

It was in 1896 that the Company of Free Fishers and Dredgers was reconstituted under the Companies Act as the Whitstable Oyster Fishery Company, a public company set up with capital of £250,000. This was divided into 25,000 shares of £10 each, each member of the Company of Free Fishers and Dredgers being allotted 20 shares.

The new set-up had been necessitated by a series of misfortunes that left the original company £50,000 in debt. These setbacks had begun in 1886 when the company treasurer absconded with several thousand pounds. Managing to slip abroad before the loss was discovered, he was never caught. In 1894, a health scare linked to shellfish hit sales badly, income for the year falling by around 70%. But it was the severe winters of 1890 and 1895 that caused the most damage – extreme cold being one of the Native oyster's greatest enemies.

The newly formed company, under its formidably named chairman, Absalom Anderson, made a slow but steady start, only gradually re-establishing itself in the years leading up to the turn of the century. The bumper harvest of 1901 helped to restore confidence, but for the oyster industry and for Whitstable, as for the world in general, the Great War was to mark the end of an era.

Delia Fitt, at Wheelers Oyster Bar. A Whitstable native herself, and a shareholder in the Whitstable Oyster Fishery Company, she claims to have been opening oysters since she was 10 years old

"And to start with, sir?"

Gerald Gardner, a former chairman and managing director of the Seasalter & Ham Oyster Fishery Company

In the early part of the last century, and right up until the Second World War, this solicitous enquiry from a waiter taking orders for lunch or dinner in any up-market restaurant would have almost invariably elicited a request for oysters. The prawn cocktail had not yet been invented and even smoked salmon was not that readily available. Menus were much more restricted than they are today and people generally didn't go out to eat as often as they do now. In the smart London restaurants, especially, oysters were the obvious choice as an hors d'oeuvre.

Gerald Gardner, a former chairman and managing director of the Seasalter & Ham Oyster Fishery Company can recall the days when the company employed twelve full-time oyster openers at its London offices in Pudding Lane. Each morning and evening they would be dispatched to the various top hotels and restaurants, such as The Savoy, The Ritz and Claridge's, to open oysters in readiness for lunch and dinner, often dealing with as many as a thousand at a time.

This was still the case in 1939 when Gardner, then 17, joined the Seasalter & Ham straight from school, eventually going on to succeed his father as chairman. But things were never quite the same after the war. "The experience of going away to fight in the war changed a lot of men's ideas about what they should do for a living," he explains. "Afterwards, nobody much wanted to be an oyster opener any more and so the job would be given to the head waiter or whoever else happened to be available and, of course, they would often make a complete hash of it. It requires considerable skill to do it properly and if you don't know what you're doing you can all too easily put the knife through your hand. Other hors d'oeuvres like smoked salmon and prawn cocktails had been introduced by this time and because they were so much easier to serve they soon started to replace oysters on the menu."

Falling demand inevitably led to a general winding down of activities by all the oyster companies, most of which were left operating with a greatly reduced workforce. The big fleet of smacks that Gardner can remember seeing as a boy was long gone and now there were only a handful of boats moored off Whitstable. The gruelling nature of the work, along with the uncertainty of employment, meant that the sons of dredgermen, some of whose families had been involved in oyster fishing for generations, were drifting away to seek better paid and more secure jobs elsewhere. The railways provided one popular alternative.

Other factors conspired to devastate the post-war oyster industry in Whitstable. The severe winter of 1947 matched those of 1929 and 1940, when the sea froze over right the way across to the Isle of Sheppey, and the bay started to resemble the Antarctic. This further decimated the beds, which had already suffered from serious neglect during the war years.

Disaster then struck again with the great floods of 1953, during which much of Whitstable was under water and the oyster grounds were so badly churned up that a lot of the soil and the 'cultch' – the crushed shell to which young oyster brood attaches itself – ended up on the beach at Seasalter, to the west of Whitstable.

Pollution was also beginning to become a problem. One reason for the mysterious decline in the natural breeding or 'spatting' of oysters was eventually traced, at least in part, to a type of anti-fouling solution that was being painted onto the bottom of boats, and which was found to be killing the oyster larvae in the water. And laboratory tests pinpointed paper fibre coming down the River Swale from paper mills at Sittingbourne and Kemsley as being responsible for the mysterious clogging of the beds at Faversham.

Stocks everywhere continued to get lower and lower, to the point where there was no longer enough left to spawn successfully and the Seasalter & Ham was regularly having to replenish its beds with French oysters, imported from Brittany at the rate of a million a year. This had actually been common practice since the late 1860s, when over-fishing first stripped the beds.

Being a filter feeder, the oyster quickly takes on the local characteristics of the area in which it is laid, and it came to be generally accepted that after a season on the Whitstable beds, the imports could reasonably qualify as Whitstable Natives. Now, however, Protected Geographical Status, which was granted by the

European Union in 1997, means that only those oysters grown locally can be sold as Whitstable oysters.

For Gerald Gardner, the freeze-up of 1963, which once again wiped out the beds, was pretty much the final straw. Two years later, the Seasalter & Ham was taken over by Associated Fisheries, although Gardner stayed on to run the company for the new owners as managing director. The Faversham Oyster Fishery Company, meanwhile, had effectively gone out of business, having struggled for years to make ends meet, while the Whitstable Oyster Fishery Company was also in dire trouble and only just about ticking over.

It was at this point, with the whole of the Whitstable oyster industry teetering on the brink of extinction, that Gerald Gardner made a key move. Realising that it was no longer possible to sustain a business that was entirely at the mercy of the elements and the Native oyster's haphazard and unpredictable breeding patterns, he decided that the only way forward was to try a more scientific approach, with the introduction, in 1966, of an artificial hatchery.

This was a controversial idea at the time but more than twenty-five years' experience had convinced Gardner, who later went on to set up and run the Shellfish Association at Fishmonger's Hall in London, that the old traditional methods were no longer economically viable and that the only way to maintain a steady stock of oysters was to breed them articially. To organise the venture, he brought in a young zoologist named John Bayes.

During the severe winters of 1929, 1940, 1947 and 1963, the bay froze over from Whitstable right across to the Isle of Sheppey, causing devastation to the oyster beds

FEBRUARY 25th 1947.

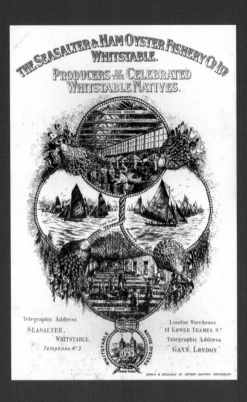

'The trouble with the Native oyster is that it seems to be born with a death wish'

John Bayes of Seasalter Shellfish.

John Bayes at his
oyster hatchery at
Reculver

John Bayes' oyster hatchery is located in the shadow of Reculver Towers. One of the navigational landmarks traditionally used by dredgermen, the distinctive Towers are all that remain of a 12th century church that was built here, close to the site of an old Roman fortress. It was from the natural beds along the coast hereabouts that slaves are believed to have collected the oysters that Governor Julius Agricola started shipping back to Rome 2000 years ago

John Bayes
The appliance of science

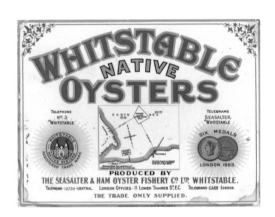

Of all the many extraordinary characters associated with the history of the Whitstable oyster industry, few have been more colourful than John Bayes. His bushy black beard lends him a slightly piratical air, there is a twinkle in his eye and his sense of humour is as dry as chilled Chablis.

The scene inside his rambling and, outwardly, rather ramshackle beachside hatchery, located on a bleak, 40-acre site in the shadow of Reculver Towers, is reminiscent of Dr Frankenstein's laboratory, with water bubbling in a somewhat sinister fashion through rows of tanks and large cylindrical glass 'test tubes' containing baby oysters at various early stages of development.

This is the only hatchery of its kind in the world, every year supplying several hundred million oysters and clams as 'seed' to growers in Britain, Europe and America, to be fattened on their own beds. At the same time, Bayes also uses modern farming methods to raise some to maturity himself on the Pollard grounds of the old Seasalter & Ham Oyster Fishery Company, which he took over in 1987 and renamed the Seasalter Shellfish Company when Associated Fisheries, his former employers, finally decided to pull out.

He learned the technology involved in the hatchery while working as a postgraduate on The Plankton Project, a research programme run by Southampton University to investigate ways of artificially growing the algae on which shellfish feed. The project proved to be too far ahead of its time and folded through lack of enthusiasm. By a happy coincidence, this occurred just at the time that Gerald Gardner was looking for someone to set up an oyster hatchery for the Seasalter & Ham, a job for which Bayes was perfectly qualified.

The original hatchery was set up in the Seasalter & Ham's oyster grading store on the East Quay, where the Whitstable Oyster Fishery Company recently opened a third restaurant – the self-service Shellfish Bar – having taken over the lease of the building from Bayes when he moved the operation to Reculver. Right from the start, Bayes achieved considerable success in breeding the imported Pacific oyster, *Crassostrea gigas*, commonly known as the Rock oyster. A much hardier variety than the Native, the Rock oyster also

OJ-12226-2

reaches maturity much more quickly – in three years rather than five – making it a more viable commercial proposition.

"The trouble with the Native oyster is that it seems to be born with a death wish," says Bayes, explaining that although the hermaphrodite parent oyster routinely releases as many as a million eggs when spawning, only a tiny fraction will ever reach maturity in the wild. Most of the microscopic larvae are either eaten by fish or killed by cold water during their first two weeks of life as they swim around in the sea before eventually settling on the seabed and attaching themselves to stones or shells as spat.

Those that don't land on suitable cultch of this kind are liable to be swept away. Those that do settle are still prey to a variety of predators, especially starfish, which are somehow able to prise the shells apart with their soft tentacles. The Native is also very susceptible to fluctuations in temperature and other environmental factors. One way or another, their chances of surviving to full maturity in the wild are rated by Bayes at little better than a million to one. Even in the ideal conditions artificially created in the hatchery,

where the salinity of the water is maintained at precisely 3%, the temperature is kept at 15°C and the oysters are fed on a carefully blended algae-rich diet, the eventual mortality rate is likely to be as high as 95%. Bayes has managed to get a few to the point where a few Natives can be put out on his beds, but not yet on a scale that would sustain a commercial breeding programme.

There are no such problems with the Rock oysters, which now account for more than 80% of consumption in this country. The farming process begins with the production of the algae on which the oysters feed. Seawater from special artificial lagoons outside is first filtered and pasteurised, and the algae is then grown in tall plastic bags in a greenhouse, using natural and artificial light, nutrient mixtures, aeration and carbon dioxide.

This rich mix is fed to the brood stock in a tank heated to 25°C to fool the oysters into thinking that it's summer and time to spawn. Once they have spawned, the larvae are placed in a separate tank, where they hatch overnight and start to develop a very thin shell within 24 hours. After a couple of weeks they develop into spat and

Checking the young oysters. It is at this stage of their development that the Natives seem to be at their most vulnerable

cement themselves to the nearest hard surface, in this case the bottom of the tank. At this stage, they are tiny but perfectly formed oysters, only about 0.3mm in size. As soon as the spat has settled, it is scraped off the bottom of the tank and transferred to the big cylindrical glass containers, known as 'upwellers', where a bubbling upward flow of water keeps the young oysters in constant movement. Fed continuously on the same algae-rich soup, they are regularly graded and washed to encourage rapid growth.

They will remain here until they reach 3mm in diameter, at which point they are moved into larger upwellers, where the temperature of the water is lowered to acclimatise them to life in the open tanks in the nursery outside. From there they go to the Pollard grounds and the inshore banks where, once again, modern labour-saving methods of farming have been introduced. Instead of being laid on the seabed to fatten, the cultivated oysters are put in mesh bags and placed on trestles in shallow water, allowing free circulation of water and food without risk of loss through dispersal or predation. Those that have grown to market size out on the traditional beds are harvested with a special system that involves using water jets to wash the oysters gently into the dredge rather than dragging the dredges along the bottom, thereby avoiding damage to the oysters and the beds.

At a time when fish farming, especially of salmon, has come under fire from those who liken it to the battery farming of chickens, with suggestions of risks to the environment, Bayes is at pains to point out that mollusc farming is quite different. "What we are doing is sound, sustainable and environmentally friendly," he explains. "Shellfish actually help to clean the sea."

Meanwhile, artificial breeding of the Native oyster on a commercial scale remains the Holy Grail. After 37 years of trying, Bayes has still not quite managed to crack the secret, but he hasn't given up. Credited by many as the one man who kept the oyster industry going in Whitstable at a time when everybody else had given up on it, his enthusiasm seems to be purely professional, since he doesn't eat oysters himself.

Ironically, he's allergic to them.

VIP customers would
be invited by the
Whitstable Oyster
Fishery Company to
help celebrate the
arrival of the first
oysters of the new
season (right).
Ernest 'Ogie' Laker
(above), oysterman
and harbour foreman
from 1963 to 1979,
another legendary
Whitstable character

'The oyster industry hit an unsustainable peak from 1850 to 1865. It went downhill from then on.'

Dr Clive Askew, Deputy Director of the Shellfish Association.

Signs of decay on the creek at Faversham, where the once thriving local oyster industry had collapsed completely by the 1960s

Sex and the single oyster
The facts of life

As a doctor of marine biology, deputy director of the Shellfish Association and a pioneer member of John Bayes' hatchery team, Dr Clive Askew knows pretty much all there is to know about oysters. But even he can't fully explain the temperamental and unpredictable nature of the Whitstable Native.

In purely biological terms, the oyster is a highly complex organism. A bivalve mollusc, it has two hinged shells, or valves, connected by an elastic ligament that is controlled by an incredibly powerful muscle. This adductor muscle is activated by sensors that detect small changes in light and any slight movement that might herald the approach of danger, immediately causing the two shells to snap shut with considerable force. The Whitstable Museum includes a famous photograph, supposedly genuine, showing two dead mice clamped between the half-closed shells of a single large Native.

Although the sex life of the oyster itself is rather interesting – a hermaphrodite, it changes regularly from male to female during its life – its fabled reputation as an aphrodisiac has no proven scientific

In the years leading up to the Great War, the Whitstable beds were still producing around 20 million oysters a year for the market. This was just a quarter of what had been going up to Billingsgate 50 years earlier

basis. It does, however, contain healthy amounts of zinc and various neuro-active substances such as dopamine, that can stimulate the nerve endings. And, like all seafood, it also contains high amounts of phosphorous and iodine, which are believed to enhance stamina. That, in particular, may help to explain why Casanova liked to start the day with fifty oysters, enjoyed in the bathtub with his mistress of the moment. Apart from all that, its supposed effect on the libido probably has more to do with the oyster's physiology – its look, its consistency and the manner in which it is eaten.

Altogether there are nearly one hundred known species of oyster. Among the most common of these, the Native – Ostrea edulis – is flat and round, its fan of yearly growth rings clearly visible, while the Pacific, the Portuguese and the American, all of which belong to the Crassostrea group, are larger, more oblong and chunky in shape, with a much deeper lower shell.

Ostrea edulis can actually be found at various places all the way down from Norway to Morocco and the Mediterranean, while the Portuguese comes from an area off the Iberian coast, the

American from along the Atlantic coast of the United States and the Pacific or Rock oyster from the waters around Japan and Korea.

Although the farmed Pacific oyster thrives in British waters, it was not thought possible for it to breed here in the wild because of the low water temperatures. There have, however, been definite signs recently of natural spatting out on the Whitstable beds; further possible evidence, it would seem, of global warming.

Certainly, we no longer seem to have winters like the ones that regularly devastated the oyster industry up until 40 years ago, 1963 being the last time the sea froze over. Younger generations, looking at some of the more spectacular pictures of past freeze-ups that are on display on the walls of the Whitstable Oyster Fishery Company's new East Quay Shellfish Bar must find it hard to believe that things were ever quite that severe here.

The precise reasons for the total unpredictability of the Native oyster's breeding cycle in the wild, and its resistance to artificial cultivation in the hatchery, remain a mystery. As part of a Native Oyster Species Action Plan, the Shellfish Association is currently

investigating everything from stress levels on nursery beds to the intricacies of the oyster's immune system, in a series of experimental research programmes aimed at trying to find the answers to this ongoing problem.

According to Dr Askew, declining stocks had already started to be a cause of concern as long ago as 1866, when a massive Committee of Inquiry was launched into the state of Britain's sea fisheries in the wake of the mid-century boom that eventually left the wild oyster beds seriously depleted, necessitating the import of one-year-old 'brood' oysters and two-year-old 'half-ware' from elsewhere for the first time. Even before that, there had been reports of occasional oyster famines as far back as the early part of the 17th century.

All these problems stemmed from the unreliability of the spawning process. The boom of the mid-Victorian years was prompted largely by two years of quite exceptional 'spat fall' during the 1850s. These so-called 'confetti' falls helped to create a rapidly expanding industry that was simply not sustainable at the same

level through the lean years that followed before the next heavy falls occurred, just as unaccountably, in 1896 and again in 1901.

By this time, the Whitstable Oyster Fishery Company had been re-constituted as a public company, a significant development that reflected the tougher economic conditions that now existed, and which involved a very fundamental change in traditional working practices. Instead of being Freemen, admitted as apprentices to membership of the Company and with a share of the profits, a greatly reduced number of dredgermen were now employed full-time and on a set wage.

Whitstable, dubbed 'Oyster-opolis' by one newspaper in 1885, nevertheless continued to thrive. In the years leading up to the Great War, the Whitstable beds were still producing around 20 million oysters a year for the market. This was just a quarter of what had been going up to Billingsgate 50 years earlier, but quality was more important than quantity now that oysters had become an expensive luxury – up to 18 shillings a hundred compared to just fourpence a dozen in 1850. And Whitstable Natives, the pick of which were

known as 'Royals' after Queen Victoria bestowed a Royal Appointment on the Whitstable Oyster Fishery Company in 1894, were universally acknowledged to be the best of all.

The Great War marked another major watershed. In 1920 and 1921, just as the industry was struggling to get back on its feet, the beds were hit by the so-called 'Black Death'. Over the course of two successive seasons, this wiped out three-quarters of the entire stock. Huge piles of dead, empty shells piled up on the beach, a sad testimony to the mysterious devastation that was at first blamed on pollution from large quantities of surplus TNT that had been dumped at sea after the war, but which was later found to have been caused by a parasite that had come in with some American oysters that had been used to re-stock the beds.

The long-term effects of this calamity were disastrous. No longer able to see any real future for themselves in an industry that was becoming increasingly dogged by the threat of lay-offs and unemployment, dredgermen whose families had been working the beds for generations, started looking for alternative ways to make a living. There was even a spate of emigration, mostly to Canada.

At the same time, the companies themselves were struggling to survive and from then on a steadily accelerating decline set in until, by the mid-1970s, the local industry was barely ticking over and the Whitstable Native oyster was virtually extinct. While the Seasalter & Ham was experimenting with artificially reared Rock oysters, the Whitstable Oyster Fishery Company had been reduced to just one part-time employee and was simply purifying oysters that had actually come from beds in the West Country. Its own beds in Whitstable had not been farmed for years.

An air of decay was starting to hang over the once-proud Royal Native Oyster Stores and there seemed a real danger that the Whitstable Oyster Fishery Company would go the same way as its equivalent at Faversham, where Oyster Bay House has been taken over and converted into offices while other buildings now stand gaunt and derelict among some of the rotting hulks that have settled into the low-tide mud of the Creek.

Happily, however, salvation was at hand.

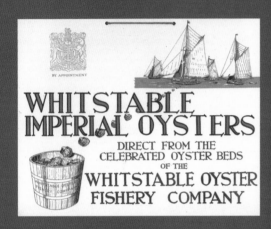

'We didn't have to make instant decisions about what to do with the company. We just bided our time.'

Barrie Green, director of the Whitstable Oyster Fishery Company

Barrie Green in the
offices of the
Whitstable Oyster
Fishery Company at
the Royal Native
Oyster Stores

48|49

GANN H.	BOUGHTON	3.
-do- F.	ROYAL	2073
-do- F. (Private)	SYDENHAM	
GARDNER G.A. Heath	CROWBOROUGH	
-do- H. Artillery College	WOOLWICH	
GREEN CAPT.	NEWICK	15.
HARRISON H.S.	CANTERBURY	
HOLBROOK W	CHATHAM	255
HUMIDINE LTD.	EAST.	4055
HAYS, AKERS & HAYS	CITY	
JENNINGS & GRAY Architects & Surveyors	CANTERBURY	
LONDON COUNTY & WESTMINSTER BANK	WHITSTABLE	
LLOYDS BANK	-do-	
LANDER DR	BURNHAM-on-...	
MOWLL & MOWLL	CANTERBURY	
-do-	CENTRAL	
-do-	DOVER	
MARKWELL	WHITSTABLE	
MASON PERCY & Cº	CITY	8888
NASH E.T.	CITY	9101
NISBET E.G.	LONDON WALL	5296
OVERTON LTD.	VICTORIA	3774
OYSTER FISHERY	WHITSTABLE	
POLICE STATION	WHITSTABLE	6
RAYNER W.A & Cº	CENTRAL	2124
RIGDEN'S GARAGE	WHITSTABLE	68
SIGNAL STATION, DUNGENESS	LYDD	
SOUTHERN RLY. - TOWN STATION	WHITSTABLE	160
SAVOY HOTEL	GERRARD	4343
SIMPSONS RESTAURANT	REGENT	6480
-do- (Manager's Office)	GERRARD	4352
SCAMMELL M.	WHITSTABLE	125
SELLERS, ALLT & GLOCK	CITY	2260
SEASALTER Cº LONDON	ROYAL	
TILLEY & Cº	WHITSTABLE	30
TABOR G. LTD	-do-	19
TOOLEY	-do-	114
TOLPUTT & Cº	FOLKESTONE / DOVER	71
V THRESH & PEALL	CITY	
WESTMINSTER BANK	WHITSTABLE	

ANDERSON & Cº	WHITSTABLE	58.
BERKELEY HOTEL	GERRARD	4321
BRANNAN. WHITE & CHARLTON	CENTRAL	5241
BRANNAN, C. (Private)	SUTTON	46.
BOARD of AGRICULTURE	VICTORIA	8700
BOULTING J & SONS	MUSEUM	3882
BROOKS W.T.	WHITSTABLE	97
-do-	CANTERBURY	553
BIGGLESTON H.M & SONS	-do-	17
BRABY & WALLER	GERRARD	2209
CAFE ROYAL	GERRARD	1223
-do- MONICO	-do-	2012
CHARING CROSS HOTEL	-do- (Private)	8025
COURT BROS	CANTERBURY	4.
COX W.J. & SONS	WHITSTABLE	226
COOKS GARAGE	-do-	158
CAPITAL & COUNTIES BANK	-do-	149
CRUNDALL Wm.	DOVER	204
DAWSON HIGGINS	KENSINGTON	3698
DALY H.L.	WHITSTABLE	84
DANIELS BROS (Whitstable) LTD.	-do-	71
DANIELS A.W.	-do-	36
DUKE of CUMBERLAND	-do-	31
EAST KENT HOTEL	WHITSTABLE	18
EATON R.W & Cº	LONDON WALL	3020
FRASCATI RESTAURANT (Manager)	MUSEUM	5700
-do- (Sec. & Account Dept)	-do-	6154
FISHMONGERS' Cº	CENTRAL	8373

Barrie Green
A respect for tradition

As a boy growing up in the Dorset seaside town of Weymouth, Barrie Green would spend every spare moment in his dinghy, often sailing off on fishing and shrimping expeditions around the bay. On summer days, he and teenage friends would sometimes go ashore at a favourite little cove, light a makeshift barbecue and cook their catch right there on the beach.

Not surprisingly, such idyllic boyhood experiences left him with an enduring love of the seaside and a great appetite for fresh-caught fish, especially shellfish. Easy, then, to understand why he might have felt drawn to Whitstable. Initially, however, it was something rather more mundane that took him there.

Together with his long-time business partner, John Knight, Green had built up a chain of 18 D-I-Y shops in the South East during the late 1960s and early 1970s, including one in Whitstable, where they also owned a warehouse, located just behind the Royal Native Oyster Stores. Later, having gradually sold off the D-I-Y shops, they developed various other business and property interests, including a specialist ceramic tile shop that still operates very successfully out of the old warehouse. By that time, Green had decided to settle in Whitstable, buying a house on Island Wall.

Both he and John Knight had a taste for oysters and they would occasionally pop round the corner to the Royal Native Oyster Stores to buy a few dozen direct from stores foreman Bill Warner, who was, by then, the only remaining employee at the Whitstable Oyster Fishery Company. A crusty old character, with a gammy leg and a talent for the sort of creative swearing that could bring a blush to the cheek of a Billingsgate fish porter, Warner delighted in telling anybody who cared to listen to him that the true Royal Whitstable Native was already a thing of the past, and that once he retired it would disappear for ever.

"The oysters that are being sold from here as Whitstable Natives are all taken from beds hundreds of miles away in Devon and Cornwall," he told the Daily Express newspaper in 1973. "None have been bred here on the Whitstable beds since 1963. They are merely purified and distributed here."

Recalling a time when former Prime Minister Edward Heath, lying off Whitstable in his yacht Morning Cloud, had sent ashore for a supply of oysters, and how the Soviet leader Alexei Kosygin, during a state visit to the town, had told him through an interpreter that Whitstable Natives were still the best in the world, Warner added with a growl: "Nobody else is qualified or willing to take over my job, so when it all packs up and I'm gone, the Whitstable oyster will be as dead as a dodo."

The majority shareholder in the Whitstable Oyster Fishery Company at this time was an equally colourful character called W.E. 'Preacher' Jones. He had built up his controlling interest over many years by buying shares from the families of local fishermen who were only too happy to get rid of what had become a fairly worthless investment that had not paid a dividend since 1928. His efforts to revive the Company had been unsuccessful and in 1976, by which time he was well into his eighties, Jones decided he'd had enough. He offered his shares for sale and, at this point, Barrie Green and John Knight stepped forward to take on the challenge.

From a purely business point of view it did not seem to be an awfully good deal. At the annual shareholders' meeting in 1975, it had been revealed, amid angry exchanges, that the company had been trading at a loss for years, had amassed total debts of nearly £40,000 and owned equipment valued at a mere £342. It came with a main building that was virtually derelict and a few rickety beach huts. In some ways, Bill Warner was probably its most valuable asset.

As cantankerous as ever, old Bill was convinced that the new owners would wind up the oyster business, bulldoze the Royal Native Oyster Stores and put up a block of apartments in its place. Although this was an option that might have appealed to any hard-nosed businessman worth his salt, Green and Knight had actually decided to go ahead and buy the Company mainly because they were genuinely fascinated by its history, and because they liked the idea of trying to preserve some of the age-old traditions of the oyster industry. As far as they were concerned, there was something about the boxes full of hand-written ledgers, legal scrolls and yellowing,

sealed documents in the Company's archives, some of them dating back to the 18th century, that commanded respect.

At the same time, sepia-tinted photographs, old posters and a host of other memorabilia provided a compelling visual record of the company in its heyday. Ancient, weather-beaten dredgermen with heavy moustaches were pictured going about their work in voluminous oilskins, while well-dressed gents in flat caps and trilbies celebrated the opening of a new season with oysters and champagne on board the boats. There were fading snaps of smiling Victorian girls in bonnets, blouses and ankle-length skirts, shouting their wares from street-corner stalls. Richard Dimbleby visited the town in the 1950s for his radio show, Down Your Way, while the film star Jack Hawkins is still remembered as one of the celebrities regularly invited down by the management of Sheekey's restaurant in London to see in the new oyster season.

Here was a wealth of evidence to show how the oyster industry – and the Whitstable Oyster Fishery Company in particular – had defined the local community's identity over the years. Barrie Green,

especially, felt that this was an important and potentially valuable historical connection that must not be severed. "We were fortunate in that we had plenty of other business interests. We didn't have to make instant decisions about what to do with the Company," he says. "We simply bided our time."

Until Bill Warner finally retired a couple of years after their takeover, they kept the business ticking over exactly as it had been before, buying Natives in from elsewhere, purifying them in the tanks in the basement of the Royal Native Oyster Stores and selling them on. They also renovated the beach huts and started renting them out to weekenders.

It was when Barrie's sons, Richard and James, joined the Company after leaving school and university that the plans became more ambitious and the ideas began to take shape that were not only to restore the Whitstable Oyster Fishery Company to something approaching its former glory, but which would also have the wider knock-on effect of helping to transform the face of Whitstable itself, giving the town a whole new lease of life.

The Royal Native Oyster Stores and (opposite) one of the many historic sealed documents from the Oyster Company's extensive archive

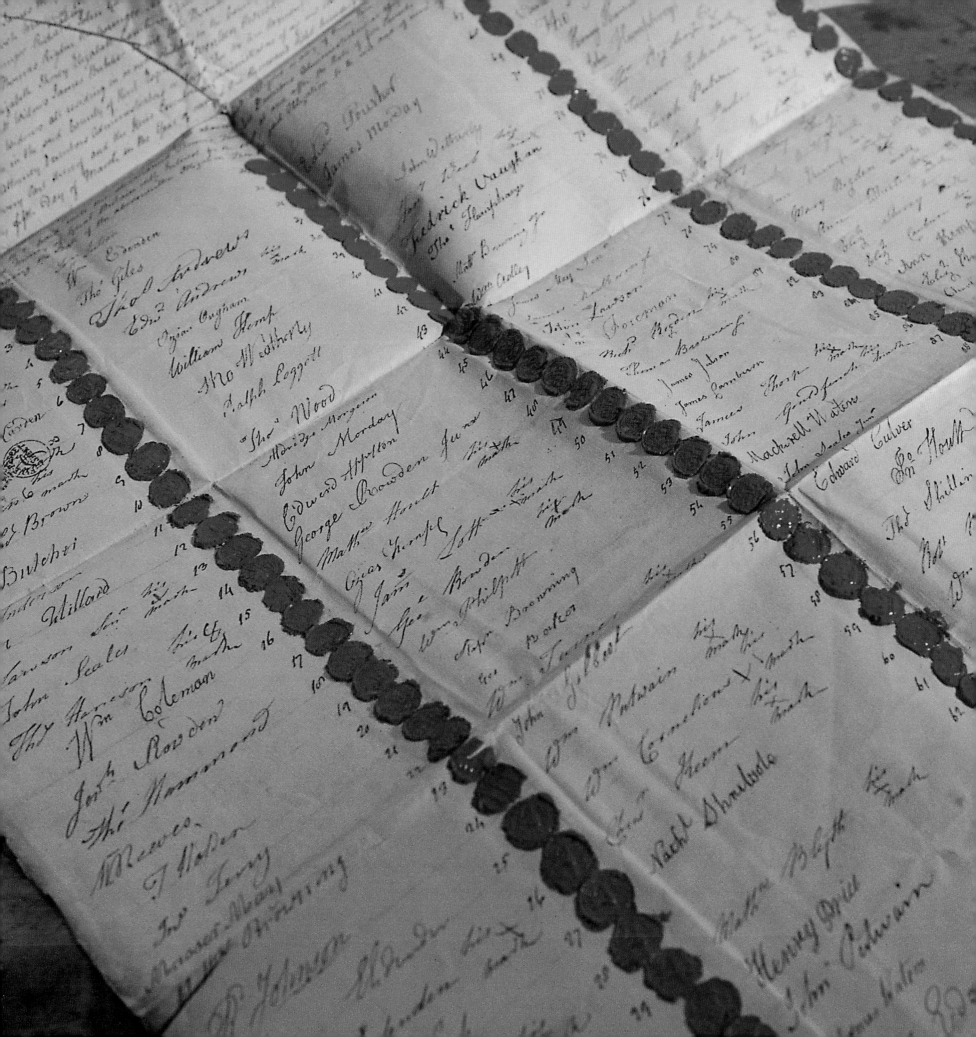

The return of the Native
Re-stocking the beds

On a bright spring morning in April 2002, a jaunty little blue-and-white converted fishing boat named Misty chugged out of Whitstable harbour and headed for the oyster beds. There, with Barrie Green and his sons Richard and James looking on, skipper Andy Riches and crewman Alex Rogerson swung the dredge out over the stern and lowered it carefully into the water to start a new chapter in the story of the Whitstable Oyster Fishery Company. After an interlude of nearly 40 years, the company was back in the business of farming oysters.

When, in 1983, Barrie Green had first talked publicly about his dream of reviving the company and rescuing the Royal Whitstable Native oyster from the threat of extinction, his announcement had been greeted with considerable scepticism.

At this stage, the revival had gone no further than the opening of a beach café in one corner of the Royal Native Oyster Stores building. Here, in what were rather cheekily advertised on the sandwich board outside as "historic surroundings", oysters were offered, rather incongruously, along with sandwiches, ice cream and

Andy Riches (left)
and (opposite page)
with Richard Green
aboard Misty

chocolate cake. Barrie actually baked the cake himself, while Richard and James helped out in the kitchen and as waiters.

At around the same time, Richard, a budding guitarist who had signed up for a course in popular music at Goldsmiths College in Lewisham in the hope of making a career as a musician, was staging concerts upstairs in what had once been the Grand Hall of the Whitstable Oyster Fishery Company. The chapel-like room where meetings of the Water Court and other ceremonial functions used to be held was now so dilapidated that pigeons flapped freely in and out through broken windows.

So-called World Music was then very much in vogue and acts such as The Jolly Boys – a group of ageing West Indians who claimed to have played at Errol Flynn's parties during his time in the Caribbean – The Bundu Boys from South Africa, a Nubian wedding band, and a former member of Irish folk-rock group The Pogues all went down quite well with the rather bohemian crowd of students, writers and artists who had colonised Whitstable's run-down beachfront houses. The next stage in the development of the restaurant was prompted by the decision to apply for a drinks licence. For this to be granted, it was necessary to upgrade the premises to the status of a full restaurant rather than just a café.

With James now running the kitchen full time, having left university, and with Richard taking care of business behind the scenes and also looking after everything front-of-house, things really started to take off. This was literally true of the roof, which blew away in a gale in 1988, only hours after Jools Holland had become one of the restaurant's earliest celebrity customers. But it's an ill wind, as they say, and what seemed at first like a disaster turned out to be a blessing in disguise, since the damage was so severe that the resulting insurance claim allowed for the entire building to be comprehensively refurbished.

From then on the Whitstable Oyster Fishery Company rapidly started to build a nationwide reputation, widely hailed by food critics as one of the country's finest seafood restaurants. The next logical step was to start producing its own oysters, instead of having to buy them in from John Bayes at Seasalter Shellfish or from local fisherman. But there were practical difficulties that stood in the way.

To start farming its own beds again would effectively mean bringing the oysters ashore at the Horsebridge, as in the old days, but that would involve re-establishing a working access across the beach. And, although the Company actually owns the freehold of the foreshore, there were elements in the local council and among local residents that were strongly opposed to the idea of any kind of commercial activity encroaching on the beach.

The ideal solution to this problem was eventually provided in 2002, when John Bayes completed the transfer of his Seasalter Shellfish operation to nearby Reculver, leaving the way open for the Whitstable Oyster Fishery Company to take over the lease of the East Quay, complete with its existing oyster purification and storage facilities.

At the same time, Andy Riches and Alex Rogerson, who had been operating the Seasalter Shellfish cockleboat for the previous three years, found themselves made redundant and therefore became available. This was especially fortuitous since it might

otherwise have been very difficult to find anyone suitable to run the farming operation. Freelance fishermen with the all-round experience and know-how of Andy Riches are few and far between.

From childhood, when he would spend hours "raking about on the beach" in Herne Bay, Riches never really wanted to be anything else but a fisherman, despite his father's misgivings. He won his first sea-angling trophies as a teenager and, after serving an apprenticeship as a mechanic, he bought himself a small boat in 1972 and started working from a mooring half a mile off Herne Bay, going mostly for lobsters, whelks and white fish.

Then, in 1978, he lost that first boat in the same storm that destroyed the pier at Herne Bay. "When the wreck was eventually washed up on shore, the only thing that was still intact was my ship-to-shore radio – and that was nicked before I could get to it!" he recalls. "I later tracked it down to a repair shop and reclaimed it."

Having bought a replacement boat, he moved to Whitstable where he spent the next 20 years trawling, spratting, whelking, scalloping and oystering. "You name it, I tried it," he says.

Richard Green takes a hand aboard Misty, sorting out the oyster dredge. Although no Natives are being harvested from the Whitstable beds while stocks are building up, the Rock oysters are already being taken off at the rate of more than 1,000 per week

After all these years, Riches knows the seabed of Whitstable Bay as well as any farmer knows his fields. Although Misty – ownership of which he shares with the Company – is equipped with GPS to help him pinpoint exactly where on the beds the oysters are laid, he doesn't really need it. Mostly, he uses the old traditional landmarks such as the clock tower at Herne Bay, the church at Swalecliffe and Reculver Towers to check his position. And if they are not visible in fog or mist, he can still get a pretty good idea of where he is simply by looking at what comes up in the dredge.

One of his first jobs after starting work with the Whitstable Oyster Fishery Company was to carry out a survey of its five square miles of ground. He found that in terms of the existing cultch – the seabed equivalent of topsoil in oyster farming – the beds were still in reasonable condition, with plenty of old shell still lying around for spat to develop on.

He also came across the wreck of a Second World War bomber and the remains of some of the old moorings that were used in the days when the entire fleet of up to 120 oyster smacks used to tie up

there. But, despite the years of lying fallow and unfarmed, there were very few oysters lying around, confirmation of the extent to which the last big freeze-up in 1963 had devastated the beds.

Within months, Riches and Rogerson had laid down eight tons of Rock oysters and 10,000 Natives, the latter having been collected from the surrounding free grounds, the Rock oysters coming mostly from outside suppliers.

The different types of oyster are laid in different areas, according to their size and stage of growth, to be harvested as and when required. Meanwhile, the beds have to be constantly tended, to make sure that there is sufficient cultch, to clear away excessive seaweed and to keep them as free as possible of predators, especially starfish. It is quite astonishing to see, each time the dredge is hauled in, just how many of the dreaded 'Five Fingers' there are in among the oysters. As far as the oystermen are concerned, the starfish are good for only one thing – farm fertiliser – and they are thrown into buckets and taken ashore to be sold for exactly this purpose.

Other predators include crabs and something rather sinister called the American Oyster Drill. Given the determination and ingenuity that these creatures display in their efforts to get through the oyster's defences, it is clear that human beings are by no means alone in their appreciation of the succulent Native. While the crab uses its powerful pincers to break down the edges of the shell, the American Oyster Drill, as the name implies, bores a neat hole straight down through the top.

Exactly how the starfish manages to prise open the limpet-tight shells with its sinuous tentacles is a mystery. On the face of it, it would seem to be almost impossible, rather like trying to pick a lock with a piece of spaghetti. But by wrapping itself around the oyster, 'Five Fingers' somehow manages to force the powerful muscle holding the shells together to relax before, rather gruesomely, insinuating its stomach through the resulting gap to ingest the contents.

Riches and Rogerson spend up to four days a week out in the bay, either working the beds or dredging the extensive free grounds

for Natives. A few of these will go to market during the season, but most of them will be re-laid on the Company beds, along with others bought from local fisherman, in order to build up a sufficiently good stock to encourage successful spawning. In this respect, the 10,000 laid down in the first year were only the start, and at that rate it could be quite a few years before there are enough in place to re-establish and sustain the cycle of natural regeneration at a commercial level.

Although no Natives are being harvested from the beds while stocks are still in the process of being built up, the Rock oysters – which, unlike the Natives, are not seasonal and can be eaten all year round – are already being taken off at the rate of more than 1,000 per week. And they are proving to be of a very high quality indeed, so superior in taste and texture to most conventionally farmed Rock oysters (those that are grown in bags rather than being laid out on the beds) that they are expected eventually to become just as much sought after as the Natives.

When not out on the dredger, Andy and Alex spend their time

Andy Riches
re-laying gigas half-
ware (two-year-old
Rock oysters) on the
Company beds.
He will know exactly
where on the five-
square-mile beds to
find this particular
batch again

working in the purification plant on the East Quay. Here, having already been carefully sorted and graded on the boat, the oysters that have been harvested spend 48 hours in tanks of circulating UV-treated water, a process during which they naturally spit out any grit or other impurities they may have accumulated. They are then placed in purified holding tanks until they are needed in the Company restaurants or are sent up to Billingsgate.

These are early days and it is still a relatively small-scale operation that, in purely financial terms, is not really cost-effective. But in many other ways it is invaluable. "The fact that the Whitstable Oyster Fishery Company is once again farming oysters authenticates our whole operation here," says Richard Green. "Commercially, it is very much a long-term investment. In the meantime, the interest and enthusiasm that it generates with the Press and the public alike is worth an awful lot. Until we got back into oyster farming, our restaurants were themed on a history that didn't really exist any more. That is no longer the case. We have brought a little bit of history back to life, and we're very proud of that."

A Rock oyster, freshly dredged from the Whitstable beds, with a baby oyster attached to its shell. As well as excessive cold and turbulent currents, the oysters have other enemies such as starfish and the American Oyster Drill

The fish market in
Whitstable's busy
working harbour
with the Brett
Asphalt plant in
the background

OPEN

FISH MARKET

FISH MARKET
OPEN
7 DAYS A WEEK
From 8am onwards

H.M. CUSTO
APPROVED AR
AUTHORISE
PERSONS
ONLY

St Augustine's
Fish Supplies Ltd
FRESH BASS
BUY 1 GET 1 FREE
FRESH SCOTTISH
MACKEREL
FRESH COOKED

FR T HEAD
BU FREE

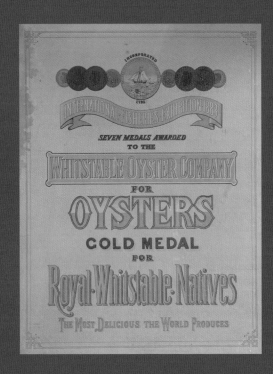

INCORPORATED
INTERNATIONAL FISHERIES EXHIBITION 1883
SEVEN MEDALS AWARDED
TO THE
WHITSTABLE OYSTER COMPANY
FOR
OYSTERS
GOLD MEDAL
FOR
Royal·Whitstable·Natives
THE MOST DELICIOUS THE WORLD PRODUCES

'I always said I didn't want to be married to a fisherman. It can be a lonely life.'

Jean West, fisherman's wife

Jean West and husband Derrick at West Whelks, in the harbour at Whitstable. Within months of their marriage, Derrick had given up his job in the shipyards and had gone to work on the oyster boats

The fisherman's story
A family affair

Jean Camburn had always vowed that she would never marry a fisherman, so she was not best pleased when husband Derrick West came home, a few months after they were married in 1953, and announced that he had decided to give up his job in a local Whitstable shipyard in favour of going out on the oyster boats.

The marriage survived, however, and today the couple, both now in their seventies, run West Whelks together from premises in the fishermen's sheds at the top end of the harbour. They supply shops and restaurants nationwide and also sell oysters and other local shellfish from a stall during the summer.

"My father, my grandfather and my great grandfather were all fishermen, so I knew just what a lonely life it could be," says Jean, recalling how she and her sister, Ann, used to sit on the Whitstable beach on summer evenings, waiting patiently for her father's fishing boat to return.

"Like a lot of the men at that time, Dad worked for the oyster company in the winter and in the summer he would go fishing in his own little boat, which was named the Davida & Nellie Agnes after

The Brett Asphalt
plant (left) dominates
the skyline at
Whitstable harbour,
where the nets are
still hung out to dry
in front of the
fishermen's sheds

his mother and two sisters. We saw very little of him, especially in the summer. He would leave the house in the early hours, long before we were up, and by the time he got home and had something to eat, we would have to be in bed again."

Sometimes, if his catch included dabs and small plaice that were not quite big enough for the shops he normally supplied, Jean and her sister would be sent round to knock on doors in the neighbourhood with the news: "Dad's got some fish today." This would then be sold for a few pence per pound.

From her mother, Jean learned how to knit the oiled wool sweaters that the fishermen wore, always in one of two traditional colours – either plain navy blue or a natural shade with a black fleck.

"Mum also started to teach me how to make the long boot stockings that the men wore but, sadly, she died before I learned how to turn the heel so I never did get to finish them. I've still got the half-knitted pair in a cupboard somewhere. My grandmother used to make my grandfather's waterproof smocks, using calico

that would then be dipped in linseed oil. They could sometimes be a bit smelly but they were very effective."

Jean's family connections with Whitstable's oyster-fishing community go back well over 100 years, to the days in the late 19th century when the company 'bellman' would be out walking the streets in the early hours, sounding a wake-up call for the dredgermen. They could then be heard trudging down to the harbour, the silence of the night broken by the muffled tramp of their thigh-length leather seaboots.

It was a very hard life in those days, with no social security to fall back on when severe weather or disease wiped out the beds, bringing the local industry to a temporary halt and leaving the men out of work.

It was during one such bleak period that Jean's grandfather, Charles Camburn, migrated to Scotland to work for the Loch Ryan Oyster Fishery Company in Stranraer. There he met and married a local girl and started a family before eventually moving back to Whitstable in 1910, when Jean's father, also called Charles, was still

Jean West picking
out whelks after
they have been
boiled, a job she first
started doing for
her father more than
40 years ago. The
whelks are then
frozen and distributed
all round the country

just a boy. Sons routinely followed their fathers onto the boats with the result that the same surnames keep cropping up again and again in local company records. This is thought to explain the extraordinary nicknames by which Whitstable fishermen were traditionally known.

In their book We Remember Whitstable, George and Greta Woodman compiled a list of more than 500 such names, including no less than 18 members of the Rigden family (Bento, Bill Boy, Bosey, Big Charlie, Dubby, Farmer, Fannel, Half-Pint Jim, Nanny Goat, Rat, Rud-a-Dub, Rimmy, Shoe Shop, Shrimp, Torysthimble, Towey, Trawlwalk and What Nay), and 14 of Jean's relatives (Buzzer, Chipper, Nelsie, Nackerpan, Peppies, Pugshi, Straight-Hair, Snuff, Snowy, Stubber, Squibber, Tuffy, Whiting and Walter 'Skimps' Camburn).

It would be unwise, perhaps, to delve too deeply into the personal habits and idiosyncrasies that inspired some of the more bizarre names such as 'Flea Catcher' Stupples, 'Dyke Nut' Olive, 'Man-And-A-Half' Dadd, 'Perfect Man' Whetherby, 'Old Blugs'

Hays

G. & J. JACK SCOTLAND 94

THYBORØN FISK 1999

HUDSON - HULL
KILKEEL FISH SELLING CO LTD
WHITEHAVEN & KILKEEL

HUDSON - HULL
J.H. TURNER & CO
NEWLYN 01736 363 726

R DONNAN ENT

GRIMSBY F.H. 96
BREIZON - SOLIFRAIS

W. HOEVE & ZN B.V.

Stroud, 'Sodden Wall' Tilley, 'Split-Raisin' Holden, 'Chin-Chopper' Gambrell and 'Hook-'em-On' Ramsey.

Derrick West doesn't have a nickname himself, but his father, for obvious reasons, was known as 'Whelky' West. It was actually Derrick's grandfather who, in 1904, moved to Whitstable from Sheringham, in Norfolk, with his family and set up as a whelk fisherman. He used to have a store on the beach where he would cook the whelks before bagging them up and sending them to London by train.

Jean's father also switched to whelking after the war and it was when he retired, in 1970, that she and Derrick, together, took over his boats – the Ocean Gift and the Floreat – and, as West Whelks, gradually built up a thriving wholesale and retail shellfish business.

Prior to that, Derrick himself had spent 17 years with the Seasalter & Ham Oyster Fishery Company, working mainly aboard the Speedwell, one of the company's two boats, the other being the Rose & Ada. The Speedwell, as it happened, was the one on which Jean's grandfather had worked all those years before. "It was hard work," recalls Derrick. "We were still using hand dredges in those days, not the hydraulic ones like they have now. And the hours were very unsociable.

"Depending on the tide, you'd often have to go out at three or four o'clock in the morning and afterwards you'd be in the stores, grading and packing. It was a seven-day-a-week job during the season, when the only day off was Christmas Day."

Whelking was equally tough, and a few years ago Derrick stopped going out on the boats and concentrated instead on developing the business side of West Whelks, in which he and Jean have since been joined by their son, Graham, and which now supplies restaurants and shops all over the country.

Of their two boats, the Ocean Gift was sold to someone in Ramsgate, where it then sank and was eventually broken up, while the Floreat, built at the local Anderson, Rigden & Perkins' yard and launched on 14 November 1948 – the day that Prince Charles was born – is on display at the Whitstable Museum, the last of the old traditional whelk boats to be built in Whitstable.

SPECIAL

Whitstable

Natives

Direct daily from the Seasalter & Ham Oyster Fishery
Co., Ltd., Whitstable.

Bill Coleman
'Cutting the cream off the milk'

The Gamecock is one of four remaining Whitstable-built oyster smacks still sailing. She was built in 1907 at Collar's shipyard, one of several yards that then existed at Whitstable

"Hey, guess what, Bill? Some idiot has bought the Gamecock!"

"Yeah, I know," replied Bill Coleman with a sheepish grin, going on to explain to a rather incredulous colleague that it was actually he himself who had just paid £100 for the old wreck that had been cluttering up a corner of Whitstable harbour for years, barely afloat. "£100 was quite a lot of money back in 1962 and she wasn't really worth that much," he admits. "But I was determined to have her."

Lovingly restored since then by Bill, who was both a shipwright and a fisherman for much of his working life, the Gamecock is one of the last four remaining traditional Whitstable oyster smacks still in a seaworthy state. Of the others, the Emeline is now at Faversham, while the Thistle and the Stormy Petrel are at Gillingham. All four were built between 1897 and 1910, in one or other of the several small boatyards that used to operate in Whitstable in those days, the Gamecock herself dating from 1907.

Bill can trace his family tree back as far as 1715, and every generation has had strong connections with the sea. Both his father and his grandfather worked the Whitstable oyster beds and Bill himself, whose first job after leaving school at the age of 14 was in the Anderson, Rigden & Perkins shipyard, kept up the tradition when he joined the staff of the Whitstable Oyster Fishery Company in 1953.

At that time the Company still had three boats – the Thomas Foord, named after a local landowner who had been instrumental in the formation of the Company of Free Fishers and Dredgers back in 1793, the Native Spare and the Britannia. Bill and his father worked mostly aboard the Thomas Foord, the regular three-man crew completed by the legendary Bill Warner.

"He was a marvellous old boy," recalls Bill. "He'd smashed his knee up as a youngster and one leg was ten inches shorter than the other so that he had to wear a boot with a stand on the bottom. But that didn't seem to get in his way. He could work a boat and handle the dredges on his own. He could do anything on water."

Other characters who were still around at that time included the delightfully nicknamed 'Tears and Smiles' Shingleton, skipper of the Seasalter & Ham's Speedwell, and 'Sucky' Harman, a giant of a man who could hurl a 28lb dredge huge distances, and whose speaking voice was so loud that people standing on the shore could clearly hear every word he was saying when he was a mile out to sea.

These were the days when there was a telescope in the timbered observation gallery that juts out from the first floor of the Royal Native Oyster Stores through which the bosses could keep a check on the boats and make sure that nobody was slacking on the job. Well aware of this, crews would set up three oil drums on deck, stick broom handles in them and drape them with oilskins. Then they would lash the tiller in place and leave the engine ticking over so that the boat would go round in a gentle circle while everybody went below to enjoy an extended tea break.

Bill has a fund of stories about "the good old days", but these were already coming to an end by the time he joined the Company. And when, the following year, his father was laid off, he quit too and they spent the next few years trawling for white fish, raking cockles, whelking, shrimping and spratting. "Spratting was very good for a while – I made enough money out of that over two or three years to buy my house," he remembers. "But then the sprats disappeared – and everything else was always very erratic."

Like so many other fishermen and dredgers at that time, Bill went looking for steadier employment ashore, eventually landing a job as a fireman on the railways. Ten years later, in 1966, however, with the steam age coming to an end, he went back on the water.

Having by then acquired and restored the Gamecock, a 41ft gaff-rigged yawl that was built at Collar's yard on Whitstable's Island Wall, he would go dredging for oysters out on the flats during the season, while spending the summer working as a freelance boat repairer in the harbour. He began by dredging Natives for John Bayes at the Seasalter & Ham and then went on to supply Wheelers and one or two local pubs. "I was getting a hundred or so Natives a day, which was very good, and the other fishermen took to following me," he says. "They couldn't understand how it was that I always seemed to know exactly where to go. What they didn't realise was that while they spent the summer trawling, I would be out looking for oysters on the flats whenever I wasn't actually working in the harbour, so

that I'd know where they were lying when the season started."

Bill always preferred to dredge under sail, in the traditional way, insisting that it's much easier than dredging under power. "You just pulled your foresail to windward or, if the wind and the tide were fair together, you'd ease your jib, slack your mainsheet off and the boat would drift down square," he explains. "You didn't need to use the tiller to control her. And because you were only going as fast as the tide, you only had to give a couple of quick pulls on the warp and the dredge would more or less swim up to meet you, whereas under power you were always going faster than the tide, which meant you had to pull the dredge through the water all the time."

Each sailing smack would normally operate with three dredges, the basic design of which had barely changed since Roman times. Bill regularly used to work all three dredges single-handedly. "The knack was to adjust the length of your warps according to the depth of water, so the dredges would just take the top layer off the bed," he says. " 'Cutting the cream off the milk', as we used to say. Too short and you'd scrape along the top, damaging the oysters, too long and

Bill Coleman with
the Gamecock at
Faversham Creek.
She was recently
reunited with
the Emeline, the
Stormy Petrel and
the Thistle for a
dredging competition
as part of the revived
annual Whitstable
Oyster Festival

the dredge would dig in deep and come up too heavy. The old boys could judge it to the inch. These days, of course, it's all done with hydraulic dredges so you don't need to be so precise."

Now in his seventies, it is a few years since Bill himself last cast a dredge in anger – doctor's orders, he explains sadly. But he regularly takes the Gamecock out for a leisurely sail in and around the Swale Estuary. And he recently helped to organise a friendly dredging contest as part of Whitstable's revived annual Oyster Festival, with the Emeline, the Thistle and the Stormy Petrel also coming out of retirement for the occasion.

The Gamecock remains his pride and joy. He spends every spare moment maintaining her in immaculate condition and even makes his own sails by hand, using three special sewing machines that he keeps in an upstairs room at home. Worth several thousand pounds today, the boat has proved a very good £100 investment. "But I never bought her for that reason. I was just so much in love with the way they used to do things in the old days and I liked the idea of being able to do something to keep a bit of the history and tradition alive."

Staff at the Seasalter & Ham Oyster Fishery Company (right) pose for a team photo

'We've brought a little bit of Whitstable's history back to life and we're very proud of that.'

Richard, Barrie and
James Green aboard
Misty, with the Royal
Native Oyster Stores
in the background

The Green effect
A quiet renaissance

Whitstable's fortunes as a town have always been inextricably linked with those of the oyster industry – and both were at a very low ebb when the Green family set about the task of reviving the Whitstable Oyster Fishery Company more than 20 years ago.

An editorial in the Whitstable Times in 1980 had highlighted the sorry state of a resort that appeared to be dying of neglect, with derelict buildings, vandalised amenities and a litter-strewn beach. "The whole of the beachfront, in particular, had the air of being completely unloved," recalls Richard Green. "The area around the Royal Native Oyster Stores was full of ramshackle wooden buildings and there were a few tatty beach huts in the final stages of collapse. All along the front there were gaps like missing teeth where the old shipyards had been levelled. The last working yard was Anderson, Rigden & Perkins, up near the Old Neptune pub, and, as I remember, that produced its last boat in about 1980.

"To give an idea of just how bad things were, my brother and I used to roam the beach with air rifles, taking pot shots at tin cans, and no-one batted an eyelid. The place was such a mess that nobody ever went down there, so we weren't a danger to anyone. It was a wasteland, almost completely deserted, even in the summer."

The transformation since then has been remarkable. Whitstable today is flourishing as perhaps never before, so popular with the smart London set – the DFLs or Down From Londons – that it has been dubbed Islington-on-Sea. The busy, working harbour, with its little fish market, has come back to life, interesting new shops are opening up all the time in the bustling High Street. And if you want a room in the revamped Hotel Continental or a short weekend break in one of the converted fishermen's huts down on the beach, you need to book well in advance. One way or another, the whole look and atmosphere of the place has changed. There can be little doubt that this renaissance owes much to the success of the Whitstable Oyster Fishery Company.

The real beginnings of the revival can be traced very precisely to one particular moment in 1993. The well-known wine merchant, Robin Yapp, was organising a lunch for a select group of his best customers and decided that the Whitstable Oyster Fishery Company fish restaurant would be the perfect setting. As well as his VIP wine-trade customers, Yapp also invited along an old friend, Jonathan Meades, the celebrated food writer for The Times newspaper.

Although he was not there primarily in his role as a restaurant critic, Meades later wrote a glowing full-page review for The Times Magazine, in which he enthused about the setting of the restaurant, welcomed the charm of its unpretentious, bleached wood décor and relaxed ambience, and applauded the wholesome simplicity of its seafood, comparing it favourably with the best that France, Spain or Italy could offer in the way of beach restaurants. Thereafter, the Company – and Whitstable – never really looked back.

Meades, who went on to name the Whitstable Oyster Fishery Company among his Restaurants of the Year, was followed down by novelist Will Self – who wrote a glowing piece for the Observer. A number of other top food critics also visited, while celebrity chefs such as Rick Stein, Gary Rhodes, Nigella Lawson and Jamie Oliver started coming in to see what all the fuss was about. At the same time, the weekend colour supplements and the glossies like Tatler

and Vogue rediscovered Whitstable's 'estuary chic', and hip young models teetered across the pebble beach to pose for moody fashion shots with old boats and breakwaters in the background. Even the rather unlovely asphalt plant that dominates one end of the harbour seemed to impart the right element of working industrial credibility.

Meanwhile, as the Press bandwagon began to roll, the Green family were quietly expanding their activities in a characteristically laid-back and rather haphazard fashion. Jonathan Meades, on that first visit to the restaurant, had been amazed to find the Imperial Oyster Cinema operating upstairs. He wrote: "I wandered up there and found the projectionist, who is also one of the chefs, playing Reservoir Dogs for himself."

The projectionist was James Green, Richard's younger brother. The Grand Hall hadn't quite worked as a music venue, so it had been decided to convert it instead into a 140-seat cinema. A set of red-plush seats were duly acquired secondhand from a theatre in Dover that had recently closed down and a projector and Dolby sound system were installed. James, who had joined the family firm after leaving Bangor University with a degree in marine biology, went on a course and learned to be a projectionist.

The venture proved an instant hit in a town with a population of 35,000 that had been without a cinema of any kind since the Oxford had closed its doors for the last time some years before. With its own bar and a nightly double bill that includes a main feature early in the evening followed by an art-house movie at 10pm, the Imperial Oyster caters for diners and non-diners alike, providing a delightfully novel attraction that has garnered even more Press attention.

Despite this sudden high profile, the Company was still struggling to make ends meet, simply because of the limitations imposed by what was, almost inevitably, a rather seasonal business. In the early days, the Greens' business partner, John Knight, was in the habit of commenting wryly that the real secret of running a successful fish restaurant was to own a busy tile warehouse as well.

In this respect, the next move was a key one. It involved the re-development of Whitstable's Hotel Continental. Located further along the seafront, it had steadily deteriorated over the years to the point where it had become something of a local eyesore. In 1995, the hotel was taken over by the Company and restored to its former Art-Deco splendour, with a bright and breezy colour scheme, large, airy rooms and a café/restaurant on the ground floor.

At the same time, the converted fishermen's huts that are conveniently situated within a two-minute stroll of the Royal Native Oyster Stores had also been done up to a very high standard to provide an alternative source of accommodation for more adventurous visitors.

With the whole operation now on a much more sound financial footing, further expansion was initiated in 2000, when the lease of the East Quay was taken over from John Bayes and part of the old grading store and purification plant there was converted into the self-service Shellfish Bar.

By this time, the Company had become even more of a family business, with Richard's wife, Angharad, coming in to take charge of personnel management and staff training, a key role now that more than one hundred people were being employed.

The growing success of the Company and, more especially, the part this had played in the revival of Whitstable as a whole, had attracted the attention of several other local authorities and council representatives, from Hastings, Gravesend and Folkestone. All, at various times, approached the Greens to ask whether they would consider opening up similar operations in their own respective towns, hoping, no doubt, for the same sort of spin-offs in terms of general local prosperity. Rather surprisingly, the attitude adopted by the local authorities in Whitstable and Canterbury has not always been quite so positive, and some of the Company's more ambitious plans have run into fairly determined local opposition, causing Barrie Green to joke rather caustically that the epitaph on his gravestone could perhaps end up reading: "Here lies Barrie Green – buried without planning permission."

As he says, it seems that there are those who, for all manner of largely selfish reasons, would have preferred the town to slip ever further into quiet obscurity. For the great majority, however, its resurgence has been something to celebrate.

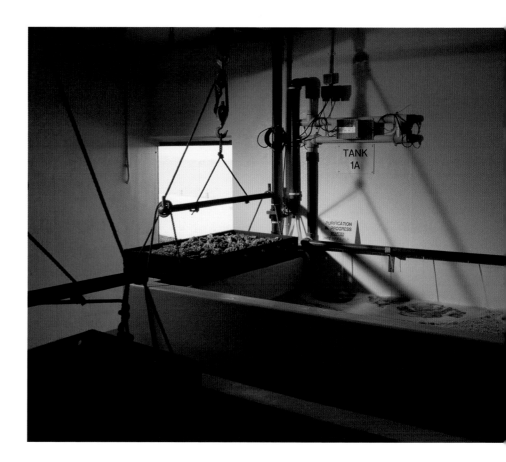

One of the purification tanks on the East Quay, where the oysters spend 48 hours before going to the restaurants or to Billingsgate

'Oi! Whitstable!'
A Billingsgate greeting

James Green is quite used to being hailed in this manner when he arrives at Billingsgate at 5am on Friday mornings with the Whitstable Oyster Fishery Company's regular weekly delivery of oysters for wholesaler Mick 'The Eels' Jenrick.

Nobody ever seems to be known by their proper name in the market and the language of the porters is as notoriously ripe today as it was back in the 17th century, when it was already provoking comment from the writers of the time. One veteran porter, who worked there for 50 years, recalled recently: "People used to swear so well it was almost like poetry! But never outside the market – and never in front of a woman."

Billingsgate has been in existence as a fish market for as long as Whitstable has been producing oysters, and can trace its earliest origins back to the 1st century AD, when the Romans used an area, on the north bank of the Thames near London Bridge, as a place for loading, unloading and trading goods brought in by sea.

Up until the end of the 17th century, oysters – and all types of fish – were sold to customers directly from the boats. The first

FRESH OYSTERS! BY WESTOVERS' AMBOY LINE Through by Express on the NEW YORK & ERIE RAILROAD. For Sale Here. And by the Proprietors, in all the Principal Towns on the New York & Erie Railroad, and also on the Chenango Valley, from Binghamton to Utica. Customers dealing with this Line shall be supplied regularly, according to order, through the season, with the best of AMBOY OYSTERS, at the lowest possible prices. Sept. 10, 1853. C. & R. WESTOVER.

James Green arrives at Billingsgate market at 5am every Friday morning with the Whitstable Oyster Fishery Company's regular weekly delivery. It's not yet a huge commercial success, but it sends out a clear message… the Whitstable oyster is back

By Appointment to H.M. the late
King George V.

From the
Whitstable Oyster Fishery Co.

THE WHITSTABLE OYSTER FISHERY Co.,
39, Fish Street Hill,
LONDON, E.C.3.
CANNON STREET STATION
To be called for.

PERISHABLE.

CARRIAGE PAID

actual market was established in 1698, with stalls springing up around the dock. Then, as the volume of trade rapidly increased, the original Billingsgate market building was opened on Lower Thames Street in 1850. This was replaced in 1873 by the building that still stands today. In 1982 the market itself moved to a site in Docklands. That site has since become one of the most valuable bits of real estate in the city, so there are plans to relocate it yet again.

At the height of the Victorian oyster boom, more than 3,500 costermongers were operating out of the market, selling mostly cheap, poor-quality oysters from stalls and barrows on street corners all over London. The best Natives would go to 'oyster rooms' and restaurants like Wiltons, founded in 1742 and still in business in Jermyn Street. Wiltons supplied the Court with oysters for 200 years, from the reign of George III to that of George VI, with the greatest demand coming during the time of Edward VII.

Micks Eel Supply Ltd distributes oysters, as well as eels, nationwide. Mick has been in the trade all his working life, and has noticed a steady increase in demand for oysters over recent years,

James Green at Billingsgate with Mick Jenrick (centre) of Micks Eel Supply Ltd and (left) Pete Seagrave of C&A Seafoods. The Whitstable Oyster Fishery Company now supplies the market with its own oysters on a regular basis

particularly among younger people. And, at racecourses, oysters-and-champagne remains a traditional treat.

Cultivated Rock oysters account for more than 80% of what is sold at Billingsgate these days, but Mick agrees that the wild Whitstable Natives remain vastly superior. "They're in a different class," he says. "Awesome. You could eat them with a knife and fork, there's that much meat on them. It's just like eels. You can't beat the ones that come from Lough Neagh in Northern Ireland. And you can't get a better oyster than a Whitstable Native."

So far, since getting back into farming its beds in 2002, the Whitstable Oyster Fishery Company has only been sending between 1,000 and 3,000 oysters up to Mick each week, the vast majority being Rock oysters. Commercially, it may not yet make totally sound financial sense, but it does have a certain symbolic significance – sending out the clear message that the Company is very much back in business as a producer of oysters. And, if all goes according to plan, it hopes to be supplying Natives to the market on a regular and profitable basis within a few years.

Only a small amount of fish goes back from Billingsgate to Whitstable, the Company restaurants preferring to rely as far as possible on genuinely fresh-caught fish bought from local fishermen in Whitstable and Ramsgate, the rest of their requirement coming direct from suppliers in Scotland and the West Country.

As well as Misty, the Company has a second small boat of its own, the Jemima, which brings in the occasional catch, but which is used primarily for surveying and policing the oyster beds, poaching being a constant problem. For centuries, unauthorised boats have been raiding the Whitstable beds. In the 18th and early 19th centuries, those found guilty of poaching were liable to seven years' transportation, and in the days when the oyster industry was at its peak, manned watch boats stood guard at all times.

As recently as 1998, John Bayes took legal action against the skipper of an Essex boat that was caught on his cockle beds and, last year, a gang of Chinese scuba divers was spotted on the Company's beds. A keen diver himself, James Green occasionally uses his skills to check the beds and to locate concentrations of wild Natives out on the flats. His interest in diving was partly inspired by Whitstable's historic connections with the earliest developments in deep-sea diving. This dates back to 1830 when a local man, John Deane, got the basic idea for a diving suit in rather unlikely circumstances.

Finding himself at the scene of a major stable fire, where all attempts to rescue the horses trapped inside had failed, Deane improvised a primitive form of breathing apparatus, using an air pump and the helmet from a suit of armour that he found standing in the hallway of the farmer's house. With the helmet over his head and the farmer steadily pumping in air through a long hose, Deane was able to return again and again to the smoke-filled building, leading all the horses out to safely.

Having modified this makeshift equipment to form a diving suit, Deane embarked on a successful salvage career. Other Whitstable men followed in his footsteps, some very lucratively indeed. John Gann, from a long-established local family, built a terrace of houses in Whitstable on the proceeds of gold salvaged from a

Spanish galleon off the coast of Ireland, and named them Dollar Row.

So far, James hasn't come up with anything quite that valuable, although the East Quay Shellfish Bar does feature a barnacle-encrusted cannon he found that was later identified as having come from the Albion, an East Indiaman that went down in 1760. He has also joined some of the dives organised by an archaeological team from Southampton University in an effort to locate the wreck of a Roman ship that is thought to have gone down in the area of Pudding Pan Rock, so named because of all the Roman pottery that used to be found there at one time and which would quite often provide a lucky dredgerman with a nice little bonus.

Too much of this pottery has been pulled up for it to be a coincidence and, if the wreck were ever to be found, it would be one of the oldest ever discovered off the shores of Britain, pre-dating the Mary Rose by 1,500 years. Sadly, it is unlikely that anything would be left of a wooden ship after all that time under water. But, as James points out: "The Thames Estuary is one of the oldest shipping lanes in the world and there are plenty of other wrecks out there."

'Everything is done with total conviction and no fuss. This is one to treasure.'

The Times food writer Jonathan Meades, naming the Whitstable Oyster Fishery Company among his Restaurants of the Year after his first visit in 1993

What you get with an oyster
A taste of the sea

The Whitstable Oyster Fishery Company proudly claims to be the only restaurant in the country that serves nothing but fish. "Even Rick Stein has a bit of meat on the menu at The Seafood Restaurant down in Padstow," says Barrie Green.

In deciding to open his own restaurant, Green was partly inspired, once again, by a memory from his Dorset childhood. "On Sunday afternoons we would go to this particular café on Portland Bill just for the crab sandwiches they served there," he recalls. "In those days, back in the late 1940s and early 1950s, it was little more than a shack. It's still there today, up near the lighthouse, although it is altogether much smarter now. I make a point of going back there at least once every year just for those crab sandwiches – and the place is always packed.

"For me, it is a perfect example of how, if you offer people the best of anything, they will come from miles away. That thought has always been at the back of my mind in building up the business and it remains our main ethos. Quite simply, you can eat the best oysters in the world at our restaurants."

Apart from the oysters, Green has always been on something of a personal crusade to re-introduce the British public to the true delights of really fresh fish.

"For too many people in this country, fish means fish and chips and fishfingers, and that's just about it," he explains. "They are suspicious of fresh fish because they don't like that fishy smell. And yet truly fresh fish smells only of the sea – and there's nothing nicer than that. After all, that's exactly what you get with an oyster – a taste of the sea."

The success of the restaurant and the quantities of fish that it now regularly requires mean that the Company has had to start casting its net a little wider than Whitstable harbour alone for supplies. The Ramsgate boats tend to fish a little further out and from their catch come sole, bass and skate. Rye is a good source of scallops. Hake and monkfish tend to come from the West Country, halibut, turbot and mussels from Stornoway and large crabs from Portland, descendants perhaps of those that

A giant Rock oyster next to three 'twos', regarded as the best size for eating raw. Unlike the Native, which should only be eaten when there is an R in the month, Rock oysters are available all year round

provided the filling for Barrie Green's sandwiches all those years ago.

"When we first started up we put a lot of effort into forging links with local fishermen, who weren't supplying any restaurants direct at that time," says Richard Green. "As a result, we have bought a lot of stuff from people like Stevie Gannon, 'Bluey' Walpole, Roger Cooper and Graham Chandler, whose boat, Charlie Boy, is the last large trawler still working out of Whitstable. The fish we get from them comes in all different sizes, which is rather inconvenient for the kitchen, but you do get the best. And that's what matters. The way we look at it, running a successful fish restaurant is as much about being a good fishmonger as it is about cooking fish."

Another key factor in the restaurant's success has been its philosophy of keeping things simple. "The kitchen works on the correct premise that good material should not be messed about with," wrote Jonathan Meades in his original rave review. "Deep fried, pan fried, boiled and poached, a few new potatoes, and that's it," added another equally enthusiastic restaurant critic. "This is not the grand hotel tradition of fish cookery."

Richard says: "For years people didn't think fish was any good if it didn't come with coriander or ginger or a fancy sauce. I remember listening to an interview with one well-known celebrity chef who said: 'I would love to do a simple piece of grilled fish with butter and a few new potatoes but my customers won't let me do it'. Everybody's mantra now is 'local, simple, fresh' – but that's what we've been doing right from the start. For example, you just cannot improve on a grilled Dover sole with a little bit of unsalted butter."

When it comes to oysters, one doesn't have to worry about there being an R in the month these days – Rock oysters are available all year round, with a choice of either local or Irish being on offer at the Company's restaurants. The Natives come in from 1st September but are probably not at their best until a little bit later in the year.

They no longer tend be graded quite so precisely as they once were – into ones, twos, threes and fours, depending on size and quality. What you will routinely be offered in any restaurant nowadays are the equivalent of twos, always reckoned to be the ideal mouthful. Threes and fours are a bit on the small side,

Local, fresh and simple – the three watchwords behind the restaurant's success. "The kitchen works on the correct premise that good material should not be messed about with," wrote The Times food critic Jonathan Meades

Starters   Menu   A discretionary
                                                    10% service charge
½ Dozen rock oysters £7.50   will be added
½ Dozen whitstable Native oysters   to your bill
                              £17.50

Norfolk potted shrimps on toast £7.00
Grilled scallops with garlic butter £7.50
Deep fried squid with mayonnaise £7.00
Chargrilled Sardines £6.00 • smoked Salmon £7.50
Hot smoke salmon salad £8.00
Smoked Eel with creamed horseradish £7.00
Moules mariniere £7.00
chargrilled razor clams with garlic butter £9.00
Poached smoked Haddock £6.00   Local asparagus
Dressed local crab Salad £9.00   with Hollandaise
                                      Sauce £6.50
Mains
Pan fried monkfish with leeks & cream £19.50
Grilled local Dover sole £16.50
chargrilled organic salmon with salsa verde £15.50
Roast local seabass with garlic & rosemary £19.50
Poached Turbot with Hollandaise sauce £19.50
Twelve roast Langoustine with garlic butter £19.50
whole portland cock crab £17.50
whole canadian lobster £22.00
sideorders - chips £2.00 • new potatoes £1.50
mixed leaf salad £2.00 • purple sprouting broccoli £3.00
vine tomato red onion & basil salad £2.50

The dining room at the Whitstable Oyster Fishery Company, where the bleached wood décor, scrubbed tables and blackboard menu help to create a genuinely relaxed atmosphere

whereas ones, also known as Imperials, are really too big to be eaten raw and are normally used only for cooking.

Interestingly, these Imperials used to be offered as a speciality on cruise liners such as the Queen Mary to gullible Americans who always tended to think that biggest must mean best. In fact, these saucer-sized oysters are generally regarded as being of inferior quality, only good for use as ingredients in cooked oyster dishes. Because of this, the fishermen used to be offered less money for them and there was quite an outcry when it was discovered that they were being sold on to the cruise liners at an inflated price.

Although most people these days are satisfied with a dozen oysters, gourmet history is littered with alarming examples of conspicuous over-consumption. Although not quite up to Roman Emperor Vitellius' reported 1,000 at a sitting, the 19th-century German Chancellor Bismarck claimed to have got through 12 dozen on one occasion, while A.P. F (Percy) Chapman, Kent and England cricket captain in the 1920s, racked up an impressive score of 280

in front of witnesses.

Whitstable Oyster Stout
The perfect accompaniment

Now that it has an
in-house brewery, the
Whitstable Oyster
Fishery Company is
able to recommend
its own Oyster Stout
as the ideal
accompaniment to a
plate of oysters

Anyone who fancies having a go at outscoring Percy Chapman and those other legendary big hitters should bear in mind that what you drink with your oysters is very important. Oysters tend to slip down a treat with champagne, chilled white wine or Guinness, but can react most unpleasantly when mixed with spirits of any kind, especially whisky and vodka. In many instances, this is thought to account for the ill effects that are unfairly blamed on a 'dodgy' oyster.

One very healthy option now on offer at the Whitstable Oyster Fishery Company is its own Oyster Stout, produced by the brewery that has become the company's latest venture. The tiny Swale Brewery at Grafty Green, in the heart of the Kent countryside, was purchased at the end of 2002 from John Davidson, a longtime enthusiast of real ale who had turned professional brewer. He had been producing an average of 200 casks a week and was supplying top London restaurants such as The Ivy and Le Caprice.

Renamed the Whitstable Brewery and partly relocated to the East Quay, it will eventually be brewing a number of different beers, including a lager, an India Pale Ale, a low-strength beer and a bitter, in addition to the Oyster Stout. With a former Shepherd Neame employee brought in to run it, the brewery has a full license at the East Quay premises, so that the beers can be served in its own bar, as well as in the Shellfish Bar next door, the Hotel Continental and the restaurant itself.

James Green first became interested in the possibility of setting up an in-house brewery several years ago, after a visit to the United States, where there is a thriving microbrewery industry. When Barrie Green then happened to read in a national newspaper that the Swale Brewery was up for sale, it seemed like an opportunity that was too good to miss.

"Apart from the novelty value of being able to offer our own beers in the restaurants, it means that we are now, to an even greater extent, self-sufficient," says James, adding with a smile: "All we need now is our own vineyard!"

How to open an oyster
The expert way

1 Hold the oyster firmly with the hinge towards you, the shallow half of the shell uppermost, the deep shell underneath. In this position, the adductor muscle will be on the right-hand side of the oyster.

2 Insert the knife between the two shells, either at the hinge or at the right-hand side of the oyster. This is best done by first easing the tip of the knife firmly between the shells and then rocking the blade up and down rather than twisting. Keep your thumb on the blade, as you don't want too much open blade pointing at your other hand. Beginners should also hold the oyster down on something steady.

3 Once the knife has been inserted, slide the tip of the knife through the width of the oyster. Try to keep the blade close to the top shell as this will help to protect the oyster meat, which lies in the deeper, bottom shell. Too much frantic slashing and stabbing will result in an unfortunate scrambled-egg presentation.

4 When you can feel the firm adductor muscle, try to cut it cleanly. The top shell will now come off quite easily, but resist the temptation to rip it off, as some of the meat may be attached to the top shell.

5 Carefully cut the meat from the deep shell by sliding the knife underneath. If it has been knocked about in the opening process, turn it over to present the undamaged side. Remove any pieces of shell while trying to keep as much of the juice as possible.

6 Discard any oysters that are obviously thin, dry or muddy. Even with the best Whitstable Natives, it is not unusual to have to reject 10% or more. Once opened, the oysters should ideally be placed on a bed of crushed ice. This not only helps to keep them fresh, but also stops the juice from spilling.

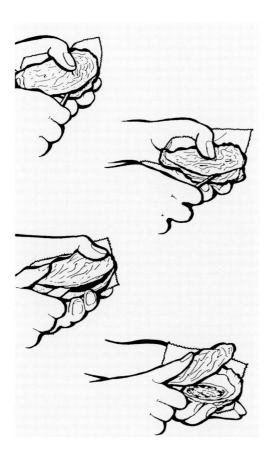

Celebrated cartoonist Ronald Searle's humorous take on how to crack the age-old problem. The Ben Warner mentioned in his accompanying letter was actually the father of Bill Warner, the only remaining employee of the Whitstable Oyster Fishery Company when Barrie Green and John Knight took over

Dear Teresa & Bonnie   26th April 2003

The enclosed contribution come with best wishes for the
success of the book, from Mô and me.

Incidentally, many years ago I made a trip out in the boat
of an old Whitstable oysterman, Ben Warner.
After stuffing myself with oysters straight out of the
water and opened in the boat, I made a drawing of him that
was published in the "News Chronicle" of September 4th 1952.
The text: 'People worth meeting:No.12' was written by Kaye
Webb and the issue is, I imagine, easily visible in the
British Library newpapers division.

Happy dredging !

Kind regards to you both

from us.

Ronald Searle

Eating oysters
The best recipes

Starting with three favourites from The Ivy and J Sheekey restaurants, supplied courtesy of Chef Director Mark Hix and Executive Chef Tim Hughes.

Champagne Oysters

Recommended as an accompaniment to pre-dinner drinks and as a Christmas treat.

8 large oysters, opened and juices saved

150 ml champagne

200g spinach, picked and washed

20g butter

150 ml double cream

30g sevruga caviar

Bring the champagne to the boil with any juices from the oysters. Simmer the oysters in the champagne for 30 seconds, remove with a slotted spoon and then reduce the champagne until almost evaporated. Add the double cream and simmer until reduced by two thirds and thickened. Meanwhile, melt the butter in a frying pan and heat until foaming, add the spinach, season with salt and pepper and cook for a minute or so, stirring until it has softened. Remove from the pan and drain onto some kitchen paper. Divide the spinach between the oyster shells and keep warm in a low oven. Re-heat the oysters in the sauce and season with salt and pepper. Place the oysters on the spinach, coat with a little sauce and spoon on the caviar.

Leek and Oyster Soup

Those who are a bit squeamish about oysters might like this one. The flavour of the ocean is still vaguely there but the oysters will not be alive.

A good knob of butter
3 medium-sized leeks, roughly chopped and washed
750ml fish stock (a cube will do)
8 oysters, opened and the juices saved.
2tbls finely chopped chives

Gently cook the leeks in the butter in a covered pan, without colouring, until soft. Add the fish stock, bring to the boil, season with salt and pepper and simmer for ten minutes. Remove from the heat, add 4 of the oysters and the cream and blend in a liquidiser until smooth. Strain through a fine meshed sieve and season again with salt and pepper if necessary. Bring back to the boil, then remove from the heat and add the other four oysters and the chives. Serve in warm, shallow soup bowls or pasta bowls, spooning an oyster into each one.

Oysters Rockefeller

This dish is said to have first been invented at Antoine's restaurant in New Orleans. We've always been puzzled as to the correct ingredients as they seem to change from cookbook to cookbook. Oysters, obviously, are a must, but bacon, cheese and either aniseed or fennel flavoured with spirit seem to pop up in some versions. Even, occasionally, absinth. And the spinach and other greens are sometimes pureed and sometimes left in leaf form. We had one version that incorporated the blended spinach in the sauce, which was then spooned over the oysters in the shell. Another version we tasted had no shells, chopped spinach and a creamy sauce. We prefer the pureed version, much simpler and more to the point.

12 large oysters
A good knob of butter
2 rashers of rindless, streaky bacon, finely chopped
2 shallots, peeled and roughly chopped
150g spinach, picked, washed and cooked in boiling salted water for 3 minutes.
A few sprigs of chervil
A few sprigs of parsley
A few sprigs of dill or fennel
200ml double cream
1tbls grated parmesan
1tbls either ricard, pastis or absinth
A few drops of Tabasco

Using a heavy-bottomed saucepan, gently cook the bacon in the butter for 2–3 minutes, without colouring. Remove with a slotted spoon and put to one side. Cook the shallots in the same pan for a couple of minutes, without colouring. Then add the spinach, chervil, parsley, oyster juices and cream, season with salt and pepper and simmer for 2 minutes with a lid on, stirring occasionally. Blend in a liquidiser until smooth, then transfer to a clean pan. Bring back to the boil and drop the oysters into the sauce for 1 minute. Remove them with a slotted spoon, draining any sauce back into the pan, put the oysters back into the shell and keep them warm in a low oven. Add the parmesan, bacon, ricard and Tabasco to the sauce and bring back to the boil. The sauce should be coating consistently. If not, simmer it until it has thickened. To serve, spoon the sauce over the oysters in their shells.

Whitstable Oyster Company Recipes
from Richard and James Green

Oysters and Bacon On Toast

6 oysters
2 rashers of unsmoked streaky bacon, chopped.
4 slices of toast
A few sprigs of chopped parsley

Fry the bacon until it has started to turn crispy. Add the six oysters (or more, if you would like) and poach until they are firm and the beards are frilled. Add chopped parsley and serve on buttered or plain toast.

Oysters With Spinach and Cheese

6 oysters
A few leaves of baby spinach
200ml double cream
Cheese, preferably Emmental or Gruyere, finely grated.
One shallot, very finely chopped
Salt and Pepper

Place the opened oysters, deep shell down, on a bed of salt in a baking pan. Cover the oysters with cooked baby leaf spinach. Add the cream, the cheese and the shallot. Season to taste with salt and pepper. Roast in the oven until the cheese is bubbling.

Angels on Horseback

12 of the largest Native or Rock oysters available
12 rashers of unsmoked streaky bacon
12 cocktail sticks or squares of toast

Wrap each oyster in a rasher of bacon and grill or bake until the bacon is cooked. Serve either on the cocktail sticks or on the squares of toast.

Oyster Chowder

5 tbls olive oil

1 large Spanish onion

3 cloves of garlic – diced

1 large baking potato – peeled and finely diced

2 bay leaves

A bunch of flat parsley

18 large Rock oysters – opened, being careful to keep juice separately

500ml single cream

500ml fish stock or 50/50 milk and water

Glass of dry white wine

2 small dried chillies (optional)

Salt and pepper

Heat oil in a large cast iron pan.

Add onion, garlic and pepper and sweat over low heat until translucent

Add parsley stalks, bay leaves, chillies and potato and cook until starting to colour.

Add wine and reduce for five minutes

Add fish stock or milk/water along with the oyster juice and simmer for 15 minutes. Add more liquid if necessary.

Liquidise briefly and then put on low heat. Add coarsely chopped oysters and heat until the oysters are lightly cooked. Add cream and warm through. Season only lightly with salt, as oyster juice itself is very salty, and serve with chopped parsley and fresh ground pepper.

Raw Oysters On The Shell

Uncooked oysters are best served with lemon, black pepper and/or Tabasco and/or finely chopped shallots in red wine vinegar. Brown bread and butter and chilled white wine or stout complete the experience. Some people like to alternate an oyster with a small, hot spicy sausage.

Use a small fork to scoop the oyster from the shell or, if swallowing them straight from the shell, be sure to separate them fully from the shell first and eat them from the opposite side of the shell from the hinge.

Americans like to eat their raw oysters with lemon, pepper, Tabasco, fresh horseradish and fresh pureed tomato sauce. This works very well and has the unexpected effect of turning a good quality lager beer – i.e wheat beer – into an ideal accompaniment.

Some Other Quick Oyster Snacks

Oysters grilled with double cream and a sprinkling of parmesan and black pepper are delicious served with fresh bread and, of course, chilled white wine.

Oysters can be grilled, roasted or barbecued in the shell. They can even be placed in the embers of the fire. Once opened, they are ready to be served with hot garlic butter and bread.

Oysters can also be deep fried, as this effectively steams them. All batters will work but the lighter, the better. They can be served either with lemon or with various dips.

Acknowledgements

Live Wire Books would like to thank the following:

The Green family – Barrie and Teresa, Richard and Angharad and James and Chrissie – for their faith in the project

John Knight, 'the silent partner', for his enthusiastic support

Manda Gifford at the Whitstable Museum for her patience and helpful guidance through the valuable archive of Whitstable photographer Douglas West. Prints of Douglas West's historic work may be purchased from the Whitstable Museum & Gallery, Oxford Street, Whitstable, Kent CT5 1DB

John Bayes and Elaine Kirkaldie of the Seasalter Shellfish Company for generously allowing full use of photographic material from the Seasalter & Ham Oyster Fishery Company archive.

Bruce Williams for the use of his colourful new Whitstable Oyster Stout label.

Matthew Archer at the Brian Aris Archive for his tireless efforts in scanning and printing photographic material.

Darryl Thomas, photographic assistant to Brian Aris.

Archive pictures on pages 22, 38, 56 114 and 120 from Douglas West Collection © Whitstable Museum

First published in 2003 for the Whitstable Oyster Fishery Company by

Live Wire Books, The Orchard, School Lane, Warmington,Banbury, Oxon, OX17 1DE

Livewirebooks@aol.com

ISBN No: 0-9542860-3-0

A catalogue record for this book is available from the British Library

Edited by Paul Sullivan
Designed by Andrew Barron @ thextension

Printed and bound in Great Britain by
Butler and Tanner Limited, Frome and London